Children's Stories fro

The Prophet King

COLORING BOOK

SANIYASNAIN KHAN

GoodwordKidz

Many many years after the death of the Prophet Musa عليه السلام, in the eleventh century B.C., there was much unrest among the Banu Israil due to the Philistines, Amalekites, Amorites and other tribes trying to take their homeland away from them by force.

Then the Prophet Shamwil (Samuel) عليه السلام made Talut (Saul) their king and he fought with the Philistines. His army fought and defeated the enemy.

Dawud عليه السلام, who was in his youth, also took part in the battle. He slew Jalut (Goliath), the commander of the Philistine army.

In this way Dawud عليه السلام became very popular and was made the king.

He was granted prophethood at the age of forty and the *Zabur* (Psalms) were revealed to him.

Dawud عليه السلام was given special rights by Allah. The plants used to sing in praise of Allah along with him.

The mountains would join him in singing the praises of Allah.

The birds too used to sing with him in praise of Allah.

One day while Dawud عليه السلام was praying, two men fighting with each other broke into his room. They pleaded for justice in a dispute between them. One of them accused the other of trying to take forcibly his only sheep, though he had ninety-nine of them with him.

Dawud عليه السلام believed in what they said and as he began speaking to them, they miraculously disappeared. Dawud عليه السلام realised that this incident was meant to show him his wrong dcing. He fell down before Allah and begged forgiveness. The two men fighting with each other were angels sent by Allah.

Dawud عليه السلام was also taught the language of the birds. When he recited the *Zabur* (Psalms), the birds would also join him in praising Allah. The mountains too used to praise Allah along with him. He was given special help against his enemies, and great wisdom to judge between the Truth and falsehood.

The Qur'an tells of how Dawud عليه السلام handed over to the owner of a field all the sheep which had entered his farm and eaten up his crops. But his son Sulayman عليه السلام suggested that the owner of the field must return the sheep to the real owner after some time after using their milk and taking their lambs during this retention period.

In this way Sulayman عليه السلام showed the difference between what one has and what one can earn from it. Dawud عليه السلام agreed to this. Thus, with the gifts of wisdom and knowledge, Allah gave each of them a correct view of the matter.